Welcome to this collection of
new group: Wrandom Write
word.

In this anthology you will find stories of love, despair, city, and universe, written by those with a keen eye and affection for the written word. A rich tapestry of emotions, landscapes, and human experiences woven by talented poets of our beloved Gloucestershire.

Poetry is a mirror reflecting the human condition, the joys and sorrows, the triumphs, and losses.

Our poets explore it all—the sweet ache of longing, wrestling with personal shadows, the bittersweet taste of memories, and the enduring bonds that tie us together.

Tudor shop-fronts on Westgate Street, Gloucester.

ISBN: 978-1-8382005-0-3

Some strong language and sexual references

DEDICATION

A TRIBUTE TO GARRY 1961-2024

Garry Woodcock liked to say he studied at Oxford, but he was town, not gown; a secondary modern where they seemed to just keep you busy rather than teach you owt.
He was an auto-didact and a former mental health nurse.
He played bass and wrote songs for years, then an old friend told him he wrote like a poet, so off he went and wrote poetry.
He loved Tracey Herd, beat poets and Ian Curtis.

CONTENTS

WIND

I just want the wind to blow through my soul,
To banish the feeling that I am not Whole,
Oh, I'd love to open right up like a sail,
And welcome its power, weakness won't prevail.

Yes, I'd let the wind blow me inside and out,
To cleanse me and hone me and into it shout,
Hey, wind, never finish the work you did start,
Please blow through my soul and clean out my heart.

Blow out the bitterness, anguish and strife,
Cut through me just like the sharp blade of a knife,
Don't let your strength fade like the day into night,
I like to soar heavenwards on your breath like a kite.

The sound of your coming tells me I am enslaved,
To the pains that so many upon me engraved,
As they battered my life with the force of a gale,
Preying upon me when exhausted and frail.

Now the wind it will blow wherever it wants,
It will carry you on so you will not ensconce,
You'll be dancing forever like a newly born foal,
On the day that you let the wind blow through your soul.

Treva Ulysses

ALL HOP IS GONE

In the canal zone, Talking walls.

No through road suitable for vehicles

Keep clear

Legalize THC

SPLINTA

Be aware

This is an ecology area

Chelsea  *Jamie*

Security surveillance in operation

All hop   is gone.

James Nichol

Edited from a photo by ShonEjai on Pexels

THE BUSKER

The corner of the streets on warmly nights
Beyond the barricades of police and fights
A man sings, busking in the noise of pollution,
A couple of coins dropped
But he's got the solution.
Smoking a poorly lit cigarette
His posture and intent is set,
smiling peacefully his words and music inspires this
mismatch of drunks and liars,
As the police brutality slips away
And the man begins to play
The ambience of love spirals through smoke rings of soul
The words so peacefully spoken float into the hearts of all
good men.

John Pallister

THE PLAN

Hello, Jim. I'm your wife from the future, and I'm here about my plan.

NO, don't hang up. I'm not crazy.

On the back of your head there's a mole like a baby

How'd I know that? Well, I also know you're blood group A and into exotic teas.

And that you mustn't be on that plane when it leaves.

You mustn't be in that crash, not in that grave, I refuse to let you die so tragically.

Yes, you must do exactly as I say
and we'll be together after this day.

I'm sorry for the other passengers, I truly, truly am,
but this is the way it has to be for my wonderfully clever plan.

No, I don't know what will happen to Time if you break the stream and live. Surely just one dent in Fate won't hurt
if it's a not a loss, but a give?

I can't lose you, not now, not then, not ever,

not 'til you're old and weary and we can leave this life together.

Follow the plan.

Do it now, just leave the airport, walk backwards into life

I'm waiting outside by the taxi rank.

No, Jim—darling, stop arguing! Not everything's preordained, you'll see in the end it'll be alright... for you won't be on that plane,

you won't be dead in a foreign field, my grief like an endless scream

'cause we'll be holding happy hands in the globe of the time machine.

Just follow the plan.

JD Warner

Photo by Damir on Pexels

SPACETIME

Before,
There was nowhere and nowhen.

Then, detonation of nothingness
Brought clauses of possibility
And improbability.
From randomness and chaos,
One moon circled.

Fury, dispersing energy into complexity,
And plasma reactions, brought promise
Of something more.
The fabric of dimension
Ordered law and cause and pattern;
And allowed numbers the burden of proof.
In direction and chain reaction,
There was no going back;
Destiny defined.
Spirals and orbits told of the mechanics of gravity;
And the gravity of effect weighed down, like grief.
Distance and time
Extended light years and aeons
Such that children of the great machine
Would never comprehend.
For, the reasoning of this entropy
Must remain forever implausible;
Into eternity, and infinity,
We will see things as they are not.

From the dust of the stars
I am moulded to this flesh;
And ideals of reality
Assume new malleability as I wonder.
The very stuff of vitality
Flows in my oceans, and in my veins
Insignificant am I;
Though inevitable.

As I tour the expanse on the wind of potentiality,
I bend, twist, distort,
All that there is.
Moulding clusters of creativity
From matter and mesons;
Using the impulse of imagery to ultimate avail.
I feel the pull of outcome and the wrench of expectation;
I sense super strings weaving inordinate numbers.

My mind howls out hunger, like wolves and dark days,
At the symmetry and simplicity,
And synchronism of it all!
For, who knows the secrets
Eclipsed by supernova?
Or the motivation of pulsar, quasar and quark?
Half-lives are lived, and unnoticed, they die;
As bodies encircle on myriad quantum planes.
Though the logic is clouded and purpose opaque;
Significance, translucent,
Shines apparent and clear.

Blue Funk

ON THE INVENTION OF CHEESE SPRAY

I was lying awake
And trying to rake
Through my memories on e-lec-tricity.
Was it Lindsay or Stait
Or then Edison's mate,
Joseph Swan? Volta? Hum-phrey Dav – is it he?

In the night it's a curse
When your mental discourse
Keeps you up over such spe-ci-ficity.
When you don't give a shit
Who invented it.
At this time of the night it's tox-i-city.

I'd learned on that day
How to add with a spray
Tastes of cheese for improving gas-tro-nomy.
Though we think it odd,
In US money's god
So assume that it helps their e-con-omy.

Who was the inventor,
The man at the centre
Of this edible type of fi-as-co?
Who would get in their head-
Need a runnier spread?
Be informed it was Mr. Na-bis-co.

Of what is it made
This liquidy grade
Of drops of just one small mi-cro-meter?
You may very well ask.
There are multiple tasks
And all measured for heat by ther-mo-meter.

The first iteration -
Immediate sensation -
Sixty-three, I observe all pro-priety,
Van der Waals interactions -
Significant fractions -
Brought this elegant goo to so-ciety.

You know quantum physics,
Avoided by phthisics,
Fuels the process and adds syn-chro-nicity.
(There is no further rhyme
Goes with physics, I find,
And for that please forgive my sim-pli-city).

One's taste-buds go flaccid
From butyric acid
Found in Hershey's, which fuels my an[g]-xiety.
Take Wallace and Gromit,
Whose cheese makes one vomit -
Not merely some eth-no-cen-tricity.

Our food's hand in hand,
Why it's Capital's stand!
Bog standard pure in au-then-ticity.
You should go eat this muck
And **we** don't give a fuck.
Check our bank,
I'll be frank, it's men-dacity.

Sandra May Adams, WotNext Productions

HANDS OF LIFE

Holding her finger, grasp so tight - first son, beloved ‘til heart near breaks with passion for his life, strong though small is he.

Husband smiles a laugh. “He’s got you now. He’ll never let go,” and she whispers to the brand-new, wrinkled child, “That’s fine by me.”

Holding hands, they jump rock pools, grab buckets, catch crabs, watch the timeless sea ebb and flow as she explains moon and tides.

He giggles. “Mama, you are telling tales,” and she replies, “The more you know, the more you understand,” and he puts on his wise little thinking face.

Hand no longer held, he approaches school gates as if she is no feature in his life, but at the last minute turns and sends a loving smile.

He learns, her dove; he grows, he becomes so much more, and time waits nary a while.

Hugs all round, black gown fluttering in the breeze, graduation *summa cum laude*, he takes her hand to help her down steps, unsteady in stride, still steady in love.

Did she help him rise to this, or did she simply nurture what lay dormant? Her clever dove.

Someone else holds his hand! Envy fills her but she hugs his bride, tight figure all in white, and congratulates with her own tight white smile.

Watching as they drive away, finding her lonely grasp reaching for another child, lost for a while.

Grandchildren vie to hold her hand, beg sweets, have jokes and stories told, her world full, life's journey ascended into days of care.

Garden, pets, children who bounce and run, none of whose energy can she match, an uplift of toys and joys laid bare.

Husband's hand slips from hers, another path cut short. Now alone she marches forth, managing, dealing, life racing on.

Finding peace in the simple; volunteering, a helping hand for those in need, guiding sadness-imbued souls to see the sun.

Son grasps her hand as machines tick and bleep, heartbeat teetering, her recovery a silent plea.

"I've got you," he whispers to his wrinkle-cracked, agéd Mum, "I'll never let go." And she smile-replies as colours fade and mist descends, "That's fine by me."

JD Warner

ANXIOUS SONNET

How could I dare to wear a poet's face
In this brave world in which I find myself?
Wherever would I find a friendly space
To put on this identity and keep my health?
I find it easier far to think and read
And wonder at the magic of the word.
I'll hold back from the effort I would need
To generate the chance of being heard.
And yet the hope refuses quite to die
Of shaping sound and silence into form.
In spite of everything perhaps I'll try –
Enabling something in me to be born.
Disdaining judgement by the scrutineers of art,
I'll lean upon the wisdom of the heart.

James Nichol

SUMMER RAIN

Raindrops on glass
Flowers in balcony pots
And calm before the storm
James Nichol

KILLING CUPID

Feelings of magical substance are floating on an aquatic cloud that is fired up from the centre of a heart loved so proud. A beautiful sense of emotional power is spread like pollen from a flower.

Falling gracefully from the mellow sky it covers the mountains with a glazy silk. Pondering; flourishing even more landing on the flamboyant shore. The water swallows up the elegant dream as it's carried down a calm stream to a fountain so cold and chilled.

There suddenly Cupid is dramatically stilled with his own arrow. A shadow glooms over a destructive cloud that pours down his wailing; screaming to melodies that sweep the tranquil reflection.

Cupid was direction and harmony; music and invention; art and dedication; bringing soft romance over lands that cried out for a spark of natural elegance... A mortal being, flesh and bones, beautiful but unguided, longed for the comfort of a loving devoted partner to move along the nature beside them.

Cupid could not resist but his arrow would bring his own feelings to a dramatic end... Dazed and barely capable of moving as a distraught lover brought a dark aura over the peaceful land. Cupid smiled, closed his eyes and love became a myth.

John Pallister

DARE

take me
anywhere
don't wait
don't care
just take me
i'm yours
if you dare

primeval
attraction
illicit
abstraction
your body
so naked
so share

take me up
make me scream
out of breath
wildest dream
view me
and screw me
and stare

down on you
tasting
i sense you
no wasting
your body
flesh glistens
so bare

hot
perspiration
skin touching
sensation
your body
and mine
in a pair

take me
everywhere
won't wait
I don't care
So make me
I want
do you dare?

TIME

Elaine Knight

WORD TURF WAR

Bic-men, hard hatted cannon fodder of the word turf war.
Liberated from strip-lit bookies, half chewed already
deliberating odds, bound for dark corners.

Nib scrubbed like a defib over scraps on paper looking for
signs of life. Fountains led by quills, dip and stab, dip and
stab, hope my cartridge lasts the night.

Saturday night delicately pursed royalty of written word. Free
flowing letters etched like skaters on ice, fine switch blade
scars seeping solitary letters.

There was a word turf war last night. Ballpoint warriors refill
to hand, cutting and spelling not knowing when they will
sputter and spit as they cut with their last ink. Gel, my rapier,
my weapon of wit.

Split you open like an inked Katana watching you gather
vowels like bowels etched in ink, letters and verbs spill and
shine under the neon sign, spilt alphabetic blood shining like
blue-black Quink. Always take a pencil to a pen fight, there's
always a way to sharpen your weapon.

There was a word turf war last night... there was punctuation
everywhere...

Garry Woodcock

THE DESTRUCTION OF BARRY AND BRUCE

The Australian came down like a blight on the land
They were rugged and ruthless, a desperate band.
And the gleam of their beer cans was always to be
For they knocked it back nightly in Nam San, you see.

'But now all is not well, there is something amiss,'
Barry shouted to Bruce as he went off to piss.
'I'm fed up with the Tsing Dao and Carlsberg and Becks,
Oh, for God's sake just find me a crate of Four X.'

And he grieved for his homeland and koala bears
Where the real men are macho and nobody stares
And the Sheilas are sun-tanned and sexy and free
And they stay in the kitchen to cook men their tea.

Well, next day at the racetrack he galloped his steed;
The poor nag was knackered and not much for speed
But she gave of her best though she always came late -
Transportation to China's a failed filly's fate.

Then Bruce to the rescue - the warriors' can
It's Castlemaine Four X, for bird, beast and man.
And the breath of the filly is hot with her pride
As she passes the third horse with time on her side.

The can it is open, Baz pours in her ear
The golden, the glorious, the Castlemaine beer.
With this fortification the filly flies fast,
She'll win it for certain, she'll never be passed.

Now the day for the winner is happy and glad
But what happened that Tuesday made Barry feel bad.
When she'd ridden her best and she'd lost by a thread
Forty feet past the end post the filly fell dead.

There was weeping and wailing and gnashing of teeth
There was shouting and swearing and no end of grief
When the race-track inspector went snooping and found
The incriminating can of Four X on the ground.

'It's an illegal substance,' he cried out in glee.
The Aussies were banned - that is - Bruce and Barry.
'So you're off back to Oz?' - Barry answered: 'Not yet -
'Cos I put all I owned on that 'orse for a bet.'

Sandra May Adams, WotNext Productions

Jockey club: racetrack in Macau on Taipa island.

In Macau and China, staring at foreigners is normal.

Nam San: area of housing and shops with many small bars and restaurants where the Jockey Club people hung out.

Jockeys, riders, trainers etc not permitted to bet on the horses but they found ways round this.

Australians miss Castlemaine Four X beer. Imported beer is very expensive and found in posh hotels.

Horses typically 'retired' from higher status racetracks. Doping down of injuries was normal. A horse outliving its usefulness was sold on to China and even more unscrupulous racetracks.

The final fate was meat, as Chinese do not have taboos on the eating of any animal.

ABSTRACTION

The dark of sleep diffuses
Through the crimson veil of calm,
And the yielding sea that undulates
Invites me to its realm
Hypnotic waters mesmerise,
Caressing with their lure
Adrift amid delusion,
To a strange and alien shore.

My mask, arcane façade of stone,
So aged by trial and weather
When touched by hands of abstract dreams
Feels smooth, yet rugged to extremes;
And rifts that render logic lost
Twist thought and limb, together.

A disembodied mind, to fly
Through time and space, where spectres cry
Of lost expanses, stark and strange
Where chronons stretch forever.

Through fluent valleys, that drift and pitch,
I race, but cannot rest,
For fear of failure drives me on,
Though aim eludes me, sense is gone;
And phantoms, smug with *savoir faire*
Raise temples, in the west.

Looming chiaroscuro forms
Wail elegies; and savage storms
Reverberate through ancient trees
That grasp, and haunt my wondrous quest.

So tangible, this land I tread
Beyond the astral plane
Though nebulous, the images
That trace this dark terrain.
Perpetual lacunae stretch,
Eidetic visions soar.
Whispered echoes resonate
This strange and alien shore.

Blue Funk

STROLL BY THE CANAL

Strolling down by the canal.
Beneath a cloud laden sky.
From dark grey to white.
Pareidolia of contrasting colours.
From faces to exotic animals.
Drifting, morphing under the sun's gaze.

Surrounded by a tranquil silence.
Highlighted by the sounds of nature.
Cries of birds from above.
Frantic wing-flaps of startled pigeons escaping the hedges.
Ducks, swans and their young swimming.
Soft splashing as they bobbed their heads under.

Drifting sounds of the canal.
People and boaters chatting.
Children laughing, shouting.
The gentle chugging of boats passing by.
Distant traffic, a world away.
An occasional interrupting muted sound.

Walking the towpath.
Alternating between maintained and ruggedness.
Discarded blackberries lay squashed.
Fallen crab apples half-eaten.
Dragonflies darting around keeping a watchful eye.
Dodging low over-hanging branches.

Hedges full of greenery.
Leaves of various shapes and colours.
Intertwined with blackberries, red to black.
Bright red rose hips, shinning lights.
Blueberries nestling between.
Casting midnight-blue glamour over nearby leaves.

Trees hanging over the path.
Like watchtowers along the hedge.
Thin tentacles of thorns hanging down.
Sparse leaves giving warning to the unwary traveller.
Nettles like sentries guarding the hedge base.
Bell-shaped flowers of pure white rise above the
long grasses.

Lining the canal sides.
A menagerie of moored boats.
Large, small, long and short.
Cruisers with pristine blandness.
Narrow boats, a riot of colour and designs.
Some well-kept, others ageing.

A gentle breeze.
Disturbing the closeness of the air.
Leaves and grasses marking its passing.
Rippling on the water surface.
Carrying the relaxing sounds of lapping.
Sunlight dancing on the peaks.

At the path's end.
A meeting of river and canal.
Through the land they flow.
Hidden by hedge and field.
In the grey distance the estuary crowned.
Two bridges span the spurs of land.

Returning as the sun falls, shadows grow.
The whistling sound of geese flying in formation.
A loud rush of water as a pair of swans land in unison.
Startled by the quacking of startled ducks.
They fly across the water from their hiding place.
A small flash of iridescent blue follows them; a kingfisher.

Hedges losing their intricacies as they darken
The path retreating into the undergrowth.
Sparsely spread, pin pricks of light shine in the vegetation.
The faint glimmer of water reminding of its proximity.
The full blue moon attempting to hide its presence in the clouds.
Like a host of will o' the wisps on the canal, the boats light up.

andymh

Photo by Brett Jordan from Pexels

THE SLEEPWALKER

The somnambulist
Unknowingly walks into the unknown
Eyes wide shut
Knows not where he is
But finds his way

Partakes in somniloquy
But no one understands
Casually espousing
The wisdom of the wise
Walking through the world
With unseeing eyes

Treva Ulysses

PLAYFUL BREEZE

The wind was in a playful mood.
It decided it was going to be breezy.
A light-hearted disturbance,
Throwing things up in the air.
Strong enough to set the leaves waving,
Filling the air with a gentle rustling sound,
Yet not strong enough to set them free.

Zigzagging across the fields,
Setting the long grasses swaying,
Just like a Mexican wave,
A distraction for the aerial hunters.
Gently brushing over the flowers,
Casting the loose pollen aloft exploring,
Their leaves quivering as the stems rocked.

It liked to play with the fallen leaves,
Lifting them up and releasing them to twirl down,
The light wisps trying to catch them,
Keeping them aloft without touching the ground,
Like invisible hands bouncing them along,
The leaves bowing to each other as they rose and fell,
Dancing around, creating an ever-changing display.

The wind spied the ancient oak tree,
Standing majestically dividing the hedgerow,
Its sprawling leaf-laden branches acting as a parasol.
It didn't like to be disturbed, especially on warm days,
When it was soaking up the heat.
It could be cankerous.
The temptation was too strong for the wind to resist.

The wind swept along a track,
Its wake disturbing the dirt and dust,
Rearranging the patterns they made.
It then glided over the nearby gurgling stream,
Collecting moisture from the water spray,
Its passing causing slight ripples on the surface,
Pushing insects along in and out of danger.

Reaching the hedgerow, it entered.
It wove its way through the tight mesh,
Passing the occasional empty nest,
Caressing the wings of hiding butterflies,
Tickling the noses of two young weasels,
With the scents of the surrounding countryside,
Watching as they leaped out to play.

Finally it reached the enormous girth of the oak,
The target of its mirth.
The wind slowly circled its way up the trunk,
Meandering joyfully through the branches,
Gently ruffling the leaves as it slithered past them,
Watching the spiders rush out as it pinged on the webs,
Listening to the chirping conversations.

Catching glimpses of scurrying insects,
Leaves providing a feast for the caterpillars,
A gentle murmuring marked its route to the tree top.
Showers of sparkling dust motes fell in its wake.
"Who's that disturbing me?" a grouchy voice bellowed.
The wind giggled as it sauntered downwards.
"You again!" exclaimed the tree.

andymh

SPRING HAIKU 1

Elaine Knight

TEDDY BEAR HAIKU

Elaine Knight

PHAGE

Twilight saturates the sky,
And shadows steel
Across the leaden sea.
The land is steeped
In a spectral caress,
And the kiss of the night
Feels so cold.

The lofty mountains
Tremble,
With a fear
That floods the valleys;
As all four winds unite,
To bring whispered rumour
Of a world plague.

Sol turns to blood
In his western retreat;
Shrinking from the miasma
Of a slow death.
And the stain of the disease
Lingers,
Even after rain;
As Gaia can no more
Cleanse,
Than heal,
Her open sores.

Shattered,
By the harsh wrench
Of natural flaw,
The chain lies
Fragmented.
And all vitality
In the wake of the phage
Is disinherited,
By the ills of a single
Curse.
The virus smoulders

In quiet wait of epidemic;
And no Eden can survive
The malignance
Of this parasitic
Foe.

And, as the dusk falls,
Like a veil of grey ash,
The onslaught endures,
Unyielding,
And unrepentant.
And the symbionts,
So blind
To their own certain fate,
Still pour venomous gain
On their fading host.

Earth silently suffers
This arrogant bane;
Yet remains ever assured
Of quiet vengeance.
For, death pledges the end,
With mortality for the vain.
And the promise of life
Will yet spring,
From the dust.
A new future may run,
From the walk of destruction.
And, over the sphere,
Now
It is dark.

Blue Funk

CANTANKEROUS YOU

You're cantankerous.
Don't tell me that you're breezy
And play with my mood,

You're frustrated too.
Don't tell me that you're easy
'I'm bad' and 'you're good'.

I see your grievance.
Don't say "you don't" to tease me.
You're misunderstood.

Now your anger grows.
How could you be so mean now?
You can be so rude!

See? I told you so.
Not so breezy now, are you?
Cantankerous you!

Emma Teare

RIVER

Primitive reason
Flashes in your eyes.
Caveman in your veins
Betrays the disguise.

You know your god,
And, well, the sunrise.
Demon with technology,
Believe you are wise.

Aldebaran is cold,
Flood and drought, untamed.
Play upon your board
The primacy you claimed.

Look into the fire,
Solstice unobserved.
Your mind, ever linear,
But the river, curved.

You demand your price,
Assuming all control.
Cut each golden thread,
Stake a claim to soul.

The water, calm, presides,
Silent in a threat.
You may tally cost;
The river counts debt.

Blue Funk

NIGHT TERRORS

Here he comes, The Mephistophelian,
Sneaking in and sneaking out,
It is your peace that he is stealing
And nobody can hear you shout.

Somnambulism is his forte,
He has come your mind to groom.
He occupies the Shadowy doorway
And in your dreams he will make room.

You can't resist his silent coming
"Please come hither" he will call.
His voice like tinnitus is humming,
Follow it and you will fall.

Upon a bed, your sudden waking
You can feel his presence there.
Does he see your body shaking?
As you try to breathe and gasp for air.

As you stare into the night
Upon your wall you see a face,
Is this pareidolia's plight?
Or is there something in this place?

And now the fearful episode finishes
You are released from your dreadful fright
The nyctophobia hardly diminishes
You find courage to get up and turn on the light.

And as the brightness lights the void,
You don't see anything anywhere.
And yet you're feeling paranoid,
Is the Mephistophelian hiding there?

Treva Ulysses

A WORD ON A WHIM

A word, a word, my kingdom for a word.

A cliché, a cliché, a cliché or a verb.

I look for a word

To evince,

To evoke,

To convince,

To provoke,

To never split an infinitive, not even as a joke.

I took a plunge into a dictionary

I did it on a whim

I found a word, a whimsical word,

A word in need of a trim,

I cut it back to whimsy and the meaning's getting thin,

Again I erase to fit the space,

I did it on a whi

I slice, I slash, guillotining letter after letter,

Rubbing out what I can to make the sentence more better.

Bits of rubber and a faint outline

I took in a deep breath

Then blew across the rhyme

Until there's nothing left

I did it on a

Emma Teare

THE WEREWOLF

It was a cold damp night.
And the moon was full.
There was an eerie atmosphere
I could feel its pull
Suddenly behind me I thought I heard a growl
Then my spine went tingly
When I heard the werewolf howl

I ran so very quickly
I tried to get away
I didn't want to meet this werewolf
Nor become his prey
I heard some people screaming
And I heard some people shout
I didn't want to meet the werewolf
So I didn't hang about

I could hear the werewolf
As he feasted on some sheep
I found myself a hiding place
And quickly fell asleep
When did I last see a werewolf?
Ok, I'll make it clearer
The last time I saw a werewolf
I was looking in a mirror.

Treva Ulysses

THE ROLLING HILL OF GLOUCESTER

The gathered crowd

Come year on year

Up Cooper's Hill

They're here to cheer

The runners, as they

Reach the top

Are ready now to face the drop

A gathering of unlikely souls

United by a cheese that rolls

The runners focus

The crowd are still

And 'Boom' the cheese rolls down the hill

The runners hurtle down the slope

To win the prize they live in hope

Please be careful

Loved ones beg

Try not to break an arm or leg.

Treva Ulysses

WHY WOOLF WROTE WILDLY

Woolf wrote wildly about this wildest place
where gilds the shore, a veil of lace
no human hand could replicate.

Where fine sand lies forever more,
once shingle on a wild seashore,
once washed-out shell on shifting floor.

Where a wild, wild moon plays the waves
and drives them on like hapless slaves
who whittle at the writhen caves.

Where herring-gulls haunt wild the cliffs,
wheels wildly on those black winged-tips
then wanes and so on current drifts.

Where in the dunes, windswept wild
grow grey-green grass in climate mild
that brush the knees of sandy child.

Where the wildest heathland does adorn
a craggy cliff cleft sharp by storm
a place the grieving come to mourn.

Where in spray-flecked trajectory

a heart soars in wild, wildest ecstasy

and a soul grows wilder, wild and free.

Where a wild-blazed sunset warms a face

where a mind is beguiled by wild open space

is why Woolf wrote wildly about this wildest place.

Christina J King

Photo by wirestock on Freepik. www.freepik.com

SOLDIER

I read it in the papers, it was on the TV too,
A bloody war is coming and your country, it needs you,
To take up arms and travel into a foreign land,
Before these things unravel, we have to take a stand.

We can't guarantee your safety or promise your return,
But you'll be putting out the fires of hatred as they burn,
Across a foreign country where the people have no choice
They've succumbed to the invader and have lost their
country's voice.

If you die in that country a solace will be found
That you repelled the enemy and did not give up any ground
You stood hand-in-hand for freedom
And you fought and died for peace
And your blood will fuel the fighting until it all does cease.

And so my child consider, whilst picking up your gun,
What is your motivation, are you doing this for fun,
Or some strange quest for glory with your name upon a
plaque?
Be careful out there, soldier, or there is no coming back.

Treva Ulysses

TIME PIECE

Am I out of date
To wear a wristwatch?
I carry a phone, after all.
Once you seemed so advanced and 'digital',
For you did not tick and tick and tick.
And I did not wind you up.
Over the years,
Batteries have died and been replaced.
Straps have come and gone.
But your face, just a little scratched,
Remains the same, Old Friend,
While time keeps moving on.

James Nicholl

TRANSMISSION ARCHIVE 1

Battle of the egos of Mankind's inner desire to be top dog,
pulling your life through a monumental slog,
Through the fall of humanity's bleak evolution,
Where respect is given cheaply to those that support a disorganised revolution,
Those misheard, their opinions quashed by apathetic social control
Caged in a world of self-gratification false ideals and hypocrisy
Power given to those who control reality,
While force feeding paranoia among the masses to look after their own,
diversity and freedom of speech unable to be shown,
harmony disrupted through false flag conflicts and an over exaggerated ideal,
media bias control and falsified religion brainwashed to spark reaction,
so far from humanity or any form of empathy
As slowly we turn on each other,
Too scared to open up or let go of our past generations of war and suffering,
Glued to a TV masked charade
Where we all jump on the on-going parade,
Sending us round in circles working to become produced manufactured role models

And chasing money social acceptance with no individual thought or desire,
By keeping us apart and telling us we have democracy, in this deluded reality,
We can step back and see,
And change who we can be.

John Pallister

BLUEBELLS BEFORE BELTANE

James Nichol

MEMENTO MORI

(a Petrarchan sonnet)

Blackberry trees in the blink of an eye,
Black and white squares on a wide open field.
Pulses in space fill the width of a sigh,
Value implied fades a treasure concealed.
Sharp angles, harsh sounds, wash the contrast of sky,
Angry words flood the mind with the weapons they wield.
Cold front pushed down, hide the truth with hard lies,
And denies with a fiction in place of a shield.

And in my memory, you are present
I delay the wheel for now;
Watch the moon erode to crescent
As the queen pursues the plough
through the danse macabre, evanescent
Whispers sand into a sough.

Blue Funk

A.I.

Riddled with errors and complications, dealing with artificial procrastination. Making us lazy; correcting our mistakes.

John Pallister

QUEST

I'm to be part of a quest to reach the surface of the earth. No-one we know or know of has ever been there. But there are stories of such journeys in the past.

I don't know how I came to be one of the team chosen for this. It's a decision of the Elders and I trust their wisdom. People who have lived for as long as forty years have wisdom and understanding beyond the reach of the majority. Even so, this quest has been widely talked about in our crowded underground community.

Opinions vary. There are longstanding fears of the uncanny Uplands. We can't just dismiss them as superstitions. We know so very little. But for many of us there's a sense of pilgrimage about the mission.

The reputedly roofless surface world may be our original home. If so, have our remote ancestors left any physical remains? Is the surface safe for us? Is there life there now? Friendly, hostile, or both? We really have no idea.

Knowledge about such things would be the greatest of gifts to bring back.

But there are risks. We know that very well. We may not reach the surface, and if we do, we may never return. Even if we return, we may bring trouble back with us.

Adventure has an edge.

James Nichol

NOT SINISTER

'It really wasn't Sinister,' the minister averred
'I merely had a little grope, illicit passions stirred.
'A simple darkness rose in me, that devilish Left hand,
'I truly hadn't realised that touching her was banned.'

It really wasn't sinister – Prime Minister Liz Truss
She tried so hard to do her sums and couldn't grasp the fuss.
If only Mr Kwateng hadn't been a Kwasi clone –
'The wealthy need a tax break.' Defunct heart of onyx stone.

It really wasn't sinister, Prime Minister of fools.
A man needs space to party whilst society unspools.
'I'm just a kindly fat buffoon – Look, even I got sick.
I've had my vaccinations, hey it's just a super-flu
Fear and loss and lockdown, that's just for the likes of you.'

It really wasn't sinister, Rishi rising from the gloom
Send migrants to Rwanda, that'll consummate their doom.
He merely wants to get things Right, but not for you and me.
It only works for Capital. Arcane credulity.

Sandra May Adams, WotNext Productions.

A DREAM

It starts in my bedroom where I dream,
Where my lyrics portray where I've been,
Rising up from the cosmic debris
To rhyme words in motions of desire,
Spreading words on my ever-moulding canvas,
My life a part of history like all of those who leave their mark,
A small insignificant bubble never noticed,
Exploding in colours of bright mesmerising definition,
To move and celebrate our individuality,
As I create a raw and honest portfolio
that drips emotion on a painted picture
The tears flood the original design
And form random drops across the abstract concept,
I put myself on the line, my deepest feelings
My artistic integrity
To communicate my work for humanity
Can't grasp an empty life devoid of creativity
Or overcome this overwhelming sensitivity
Writing and inspiring poetry
Waking up from my slumber of self-doubt
Acknowledging what I am,
A scholar, a man of many words
Born to converse and interact
Fuel my drive for life as I stand strong against the doubters
The cage created for me to keep me down and depressed,
I rise up again and again this time to take the blows
To feel the energy beating in my heart
My only way I see the only thing I can express
Energy complete
Freedom is all I seek.

John Pallister

THROUGH OUR EYES

People passing by on the street below
The changing facades an invisible backdrop.
Oblivious to the world around,
Their faces pointing to the ground,
Eyes averted ever down.

Distorted, through the condensation on my window,
Why is it that people appear strange?
Confusion at the sight,
Confusion at the sounds.
Senses overloaded with bewilderment,
Never once pausing to look around.

Their future silently evolving into the past,
Dissolving into the inexorable stream.
Summoned by infinity,
No-one hears their scream.
Sliding down their world lines

Instead of gliding toward their dreams.

Minds with shuttered blinds,

Life can be confusing, as it isn't what it seems.

andymh, Treva Ulysses, Blue Funk

Photo by Mike Chai of Pexels

STROUD TEXTILE MILLS – PROGRESS AND DEATH

Skyline scarred so diabolically,
victim of blunt archaeology.
Where once the Wild God oft did roam,
willow-herb fades unto the gloam.
Life force cemented in the stone.

Spinning wheel idles at the hearth,
art thou deservèd of such wrath?
Metal clock slicing down twelve hours,
a striking symbol of relinquished powers.
Souls cut through under tall cell bowers.

Weave now the yarn in fine symmetry,
breath now the air in close proximity
Consumption creeps in behind the wall,
no man predicted this fatal flaw.
Death unravels from around the spool.

Stroud Scarlet, broadcloth for a redcoat,
Stroud Scarlet, cloth dyed for a death coat.
Dyed and dried and marched away,
finely clad at least were they,
wrapped in scarlet where they lay.

Pale cold stone under waxing moon,
black shadows fall on surplus looms.
Idle the mule and carding machines,
silence trembles over unstitched seams.
Cast off now are these broadcloth dreams.

Christina J King

Dunkirk Mills, near Nailsworth. Original Mills of "John Halifax Gentleman."

INSPIRED BY JOAN BAEZ

Hello, Joan.

I love your voice filling my mansion.

Reminding me life is diamonds and rust and if I have nowhere for my words, I have no stanchion.

Most of life I have been told off, but rarely asked why. I'm the boy in Kes.

I hold a diamond to the sky and see the beauty in its flaw... the shine of a crazy diamond.

Garry Woodcock

Photo by Tatiana Syrikora on Pexels

TOGETHER YET ALONE

We went out together
Yet we were both alone
Holding hands felt empty
Just something that is done

When I compliment you
You show your best fake smile
I know that it's not heartfelt
As I've known you for a while

You think that you can fool me
And I know that this is true
It's been happening for some time now
That the one has become two.

It's your defence mechanism
A skill you learned to hone
But what it really says is
We're together yet alone.

Treva Ulysses

THE BIG WORLD

The World is Big,
    so big it's interesting.
It's scary,
    so scary it's fascinating.
It's daunting,
    so daunting it's exciting.

To make it small,
    it has to be explored.
The journey we travel,
    makes it soothing.
The vistas we see,
    make it a delight.

The world is big,
    we are small.
The journey makes us grow
    and the world small.

andymh

MONDAY-ON-SEA

We slip into the duvet tide and let it flood over us.

Gently treading, bobbing, holding heads above water.

Then the first squall breaks and we dive amongst the waves tumbling, the exciting disorientation of not knowing up from down.

From our pillows of sand, we gaze into the deep blue-green of our ocean.

Another dip? Yes. Let's, and so our tide ebbs and flows.

Eventually coming to rest on separate islands, not apart.

Anticipating when we will swim again.

Garry Woodcock

ANOTHER POINTLESS SUNDAY

Sunday, bloody Sunday

The pointless full stop period to another week.

Ahhh, but the Sundays of childhood.

Coconut macaroons, nut brittle and sherbet dabs.

Random drives.

Watching rain drops osmotically join.

Annie on the radio, 'Running with the pack'

Round about lessons in not getting lost, not in this fair isle.

But some landscapes are easier to navigate than the one inside...

Garry Woodcock

POOR WI-FI

You left me because of poor Wi-Fi
I really won't lie
but my last message was sent a week ago
And just so you know
my internet really was slow
my Facebook app crashed with a single notification
and because of my loyal dedication
I would spend hours to send a one-megabyte email
and even when I Tweet
for us to meet it would take a week
before you could even log on
and when you received, the moment was gone,
I tried to listen to Spotify; our song,
but the search engine came up wrong,
Windows 8 wiped anything to do with you
and now I don't know what to do.

John Pallister

SUNSET ON WESTGATE

The sun setting.

Casting its glow of orange reds.

The upper storeys of Westgate ablaze.

As the colours reflected along its length.

A varied skyline of historical rooftops.

Slipping into silhouette as the sun fades away.

Contrasted by dark grey clouds.

Ushering an early night.

Andymh

St Nicholas, Westgate Street, built in 1190.

GLOBAL DIMENSION CARETAKERS

Transcending through realities,
The imaginators,
The beautiful, rewired creators,
connecting to higher source,
to steer humanity on course
a chosen family of liberators
that follow love wisdom and serenity,
to build up compassion and forgiveness,
Ones who hang on the fringes of society's rules,
observing relating to the greater good and growth of mankind.

John Pallister

HEALTH PROBLEM

We've lost the chance to sugar the pill.
This is a very bad result.
The situation won't stay still.
This is a very bad result.
The problem came from an animalcule.
This is a very bad result.
Small and unseen it's made us fools.
This is a very bad result.
Much more lethal than Covid 19.
This is a very bad result.
The most toxic critter ever seen.
This is a very bad result.
Coincidence it must surely be.
This is a very bad result.
That it came from my brother's laboratory.
This is a very bad result.
Synchronicity? Cause and effect?
This is a very bad result.
Whatever the case we're completely wrecked.
This is a very bad result.
One percent will survive this thing.
This is a very bad result.
I hope it's the one that I am in.
This is a very bad result.

James Nichol

LAND'S EMBRACE

I cherish my Gloucestershire village, grown up amongst trees, where rooks and jackdaws weave

their raucous morning symphony, as o'er Hartpury Hill wakes our distant star, swift as a blush, ablaze and bright, fern-fringed country paths catching dawn's first light

and warmth rises, blossom unfurls, perry trees smile again as they have for a thousand years, and walnuts sprouted from Roman gifts, once pressed to oil, now grow all around.

I love this land in the waking spring, the blazing summer, the gold-glow autumn and creeping winter, when clustered hedge berries call blackbirds and fieldfare to their snow kissed harvest,

but for now the land awakens, and while badgers snuffle and frogs seek ponds, I smile at the trees, hear their growing songs, feel at peace and know all is as it should be.

JD Warner

A view across misty Hartpury fields in the blaze of autumnal sunrise.

SOUL GUARDIAN

A tree I met, with branches wide,
Green leaves that rustled by my side,
I sat beneath, and felt the breeze,
It breathed the wisdom of all trees.

I talked to it, and it talked back,
In whispers soft, words did not lack.
I told it tales of days gone by,
It spoke of dragons in the sky.

I found a friend, in this grand tree,
A friend who'd always listen to me.
And though it stood so tall and grand,
It never judged, nor took a stand.

So if you're lost or feel alone,
Just find a tree to call your own.
And sit beneath its wide embrace,
To feel the peace deep in that place.

JD Warner

SUMMER'S END HAIKU

Image by Rodolphe_SGT from Pixabay

Elaine Knight

FLOWERS

JD Warner

MISTLETOE MAIDEN

The sun drops below the horizon.
Its last spectral rays pulling the darkness over.
The lingering chill growing colder.
The mid-afternoon falls dark.

Shop windows spill out their lights.
Pavements becoming a patchwork of light and dark.
Christmas decorations sparkle.
Necklaces for the festive displays.

Multicoloured glows illuminate the skies.
Houses lighting up.
The festive decorations coming alive.
Bringing cheer and warmth in darkening chill.

Streets of people rushing.
Making their way home.
A place of refuge.
An escape from the outside.

The lengthening evening bringing people out.
Seeking their favourite haunts.
Joining friends and family celebrating.
Ushering in the weekend.

In a darkened doorway.
Mistletoe held high.
A couple embrace.
The woman pulls away into the crowd.

Her face hidden in the fur-lined hood.
The winter coat, fluttering at her feet.
Gloves protecting her hands.
Mistletoe clasped in them.

She wanders the establishments.
Giving out her Christmas gift.
The Mistletoe Kiss.
A festive cheer for young and old.

The morning light beams out.
Highlighting a macabre trail.
Bodies of men, young and old.
All frozen, sparkling white.

Linked by the cause of death.
An unnatural heart attack.
Their pockets containing a mistletoe leaf.
A gift from the Mistletoe Maiden.

As the festive season progressed.
Celebrations bringing cheer increased.
The body count multiplied.
Death stalked the parties.

She wasn't seen entering a building.
Nor was she ever seen leaving.
Yet her presence was noted within.
Mingling with an air of elegant confidence.

Mistletoe clasped close to her chest.
Chatting when she would stop or be stopped.
Raising the mistletoe, she would kiss them.
Moving away with a delightful laugh.

She was remembered for the long winter coat.
The enchanting smile they saw.
Along with her ethereal presence.
Which they found beguiling.

Her demeanour made an impression.
Memories of her were vague.
But what was not in doubt.
Her visitation left a body or two.

Excitement grew as Christmas drew near.
The partying went on.
The cheer undiminished.
Despite the deeds of the Mistletoe Maiden.

andymh

LOST LOVE

My heartbeat mirrors yours
As I search for cures
To this instability they call love
And I've had enough.
You once had an open heart
Before you finally did depart
From many realities I keep coming back to you
Simultaneously branching through.
For when we met it was a brief moment in time
But I can say however short, you were mine
Now through the deepest abyss
We no longer kiss
Or talk at all
The dreaded fall
As we collide no more
Conversation seems to bore
And we wonder why we were in love?
Was it ever enough?
That passion has diminished the flame
The manipulation, the game
Longing to see your piercing eyes.
My soul cries

For elegance and your soft touch

I miss you so much

But I know deep down there's a connection

Some form of reaction

That sways you back into my arms

Forgiving our qualms.

Picturing a beach

Where you're just in reach

And the water is calm and still

We'll meet again I know we will.

John Pallister

YOU

If I could be you
For just one day,
I would throw away
All those clothes
That don't suit you,
And dress in a style
That does.
If I could be you,
Would I still
Like the colour blue?
Or would your eyes
See red,
And make me
Prefer grey?
If I could be you
Would I be attracted to
That movie star,
The one you like so much?
Or would I still lust
Over *my* fantasies,
And find a man's skin
Pleasing to touch?
I wish I knew.
For just one day
I would read your books
And write your stories,

And discover the god
To which you pray.
I would learn your prejudices,
And air your views,
And feel your anger –
And your dismay –
At the evening news.
If I could be you
Would I like your music?
I would listen to it all,
Hearing as you do,
And read your diary.
Then I would surely know
How you pass your time away.
But – if I could be you,
Even for only one day,
I would know what
You really think of me.
Perhaps it's better this way,
That you are you
And I am
Someone else.

Blue Funk

BAGGAGE

I come home from work and trip over
some baggage.
It's been lying around in the hallway
for so long now, I can't remember
when it was placed there.
Time for a cup of tea.
In the kitchen
I notice more baggage –
baggage behind the kettle;
baggage in front of the cooker;
baggage beside the fridge.
Baggage clutters the worktop and
the baggage-laden table groans
beneath the weight of
excess baggage.
All this baggage
makes me feel hungry;
I need energy to deal with it –
so much energy that I eat
even when I am not hungry.
Opening the fridge door,
I see baggage
on every shelf.
"Not this time, baggage," I say,
and close the fridge door again.
Stripped naked,
I step into the shower.
If only I could slit open the baggage resting
on the cold floor tiles
I might feel some warmth beneath my feet.
But the baggage hanging from the corner of
the bathroom mirror
presents more of a pressing problem –

this baggage looks so heavy
the mirror might wrench
right off the wall
at any moment.
Bare feet on glass
I've felt the sting of it before.
Snatching up a towel, I
hear the sound of smashing glass as I
close the bathroom door behind me.
Next, I've got to straddle
the baggage
strewn all across the landing.
Stepping over,
stepping around,
straddling,
climbing over,
being flattened
by baggage
and having to retrace my steps
time after time.
I'm exhausted
but it's not time to sleep
amongst the baggage yet.
Talking of sleep,
I discover more baggage in the bedroom.
Some of this baggage has been unpacked –
there are piles of stuff
scattered on the floor,
flung into the wardrobe,
dumped onto the bed,
strewn across my dressing table,
spilling from my bookcase.
So much baggage.
It's all got too difficult, too out of control.
There are just way too many bags
EVERYWHERE.

I decide that now might be a good
time to open a few more bags and
put some stuff away.
Better make a start then.
I drink a gin or two while I attempt it.
Several bags have zips straining to contain
that which lies within –
there's going to be one hell of a mess if those
zips break all at the same time.
I drink a gin or three whilst I contemplate it.
There are padlocks on a number of the bags
but I don't have the corresponding keys –
they've been lost somewhere.
I have a hazy, haunting memory of what
is inside some of these bags.
I drink a gin or four and try to forget about it.
Sometimes,
I think about setting fire to the whole
damn lot of it –
all of these crazy piled high bags.
Can't, though –
I'll likely burn the house down too
and others live here now.
My daughter appears in the bedroom
and picks up a bag of books.
"Mum, I think you've got enough books now,"
she declares.
I smile…
There was never enough…
there is never enough.
But she's got a point.
So, I decide that
on one fine day,
I'm going to put some of the bags
in a skip.
And those gin bottles too.

Then I'm going to build a room
just for the bags
I don't quite know what to do with
but can't get rid of, yet.
And the rest of the bags…
well, I'll steadily unpack them
even if it takes me forever.

Christina J King

Our final poem is from Garry, RIP.

ODE TO BENJAMIN

So you came from Handsworth with your Steel Pulse and your eyes on fire.

You could be fuelled by righteous anger.

But you had this sparkle in your eye and a smile as big as dawn.

How absurd that those who thought adding Empire to your name would please you. They never heard your words. Had they heard you perform?

They'd throw a dead dog bone. A smug illuminate.

Zephania means hidden by god.

Glad you weren't hidden from us.

Write for Jah now and we'll catch your words in the sun and the falling rain.

Garry Woodcock

Contributors

JAMES NICHOL lives in the city of Gloucester. He has always loved the power and magic of the written word at its best. This applies both to creative and discursive writing. Throughout his life he has been involved in writing, mainly discursive. Currently, he finds himself nudged more to the creative side. He is pleased and grateful to be part of this collection.
For more than a decade, most of his writing has related to his blog: https://contemplativeinquiry.blog/. The blog is grounded in modern Druidry, which he practises more as an eco-philosophy than as a devotional religion. In this blog, he includes personal sharing, discursive writing, photographs, poetry, and book reviews. His book *Contemplative Druidry: People, Practice and Potential* was published in 2014.

JD WARNER lives a little north of Gloucester, in a quiet village where nature inspires her writing. A mother, grandmother and amateur geologist, her sci-fi and fantasy novels can be found on Amazon as paperbacks or Kindles.

SANDRA MAY ADAMS of WotNext Productions is an academic, director, scriptwriter, actress and performance poet.

ELAINE KNIGHT lives on the site of an ancient orchard overlooking the remains of the old Roman city wall of Gloucester. She likes words and images. A dreamer, artist and poet. Her blog is https://elaineknight.wordpress.com

JOHN PALLISTER is a poet and a short story writer. He likes to think he has a distinct style, but he ranges in subject matter from dark and witty to fun and light, but he also likes to have some meaning whether it be positive or negative. He hopes you enjoy some of his pieces included in this book. Please check his page on Facebook for other poems, short stories, and news.

TREVA ULYSSES is a poet and songwriter who started to write in 1980. In 2022 he entered the Gloucester poetry festival slam and came third in the final. Later in 2022 he adopted the name Ulysses after a discovery his brother made on an Ancestry website. Since then, he has performed at open mics and sometimes reads his poetry to people in pubs and cafes. "It's a truly great experience when people let you read your poetry or share your songs with them." Treva Ulysses also writes short stories and his favourite books are dictionaries and atlases.

CHRISTINA J KING is a mother; writer; poet; daydreamer; vintage fanatic; conservation volunteer; and outdoor enthusiast. She is interested in all things Victoriana; likely eccentric; a keen reader of philosophy and psychology; a philomath and a would-be apiarist.
She is delighted to have been asked to contribute some of her early works of poetry to this anthology. Her debut novel, Shadow Life, is available on Amazon, with all proceeds from its sale donated to a baby loss charity.

BLUE FUNK is renowned throughout Gloucester by almost nobody. Her words of wisdom echo through the ghettos of Tuffley, annoying the neighbours and causing widespread dissention amongst the philosophers who dwell within. Some say she may be deluded, but we know that she's full of poppycock.

ANDY HARRISON (andymh) spent most of his life in a northern town on the edge of the Pennines before settling in the city of Gloucester.
He is currently practising learning how to become a trainee novice scribbler of letters in both written and hand-drawn forms.
With a fascination of how words can grow into a narrative, entertaining through the images generated and the emotions and feelings that are stimulated, he has contributed a few of his efforts to this anthology.
He has an interest in the philosophies of ancient civilizations from around the world, including Chinese, Japanese, Egyptian and South American, reading of how they viewed and understood the world, life and afterlife, as well as their histories.

EMMA RAE TEARE was born in Southampton, and now lives happily in Gloucester. Between tirelessly working for the NHS, learning Spanish, and cinema visits, she writes poetry and books. "The Second Life of Penny Longhope." has recently been published.

Printed in Great Britain
by Amazon

40758297R00056